Fruit Salad

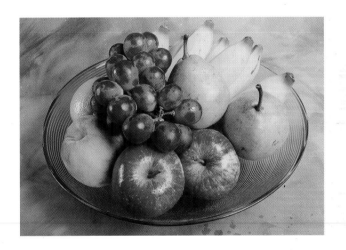

Written by Frances Lee
Photography by Michael Curtain

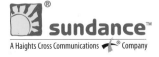

® sundance™
A Haights Cross Communications ® Company

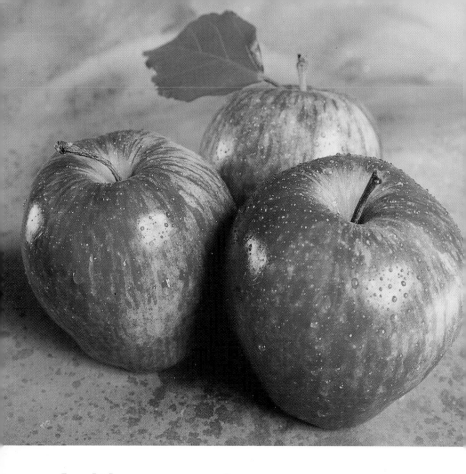

I like apples.

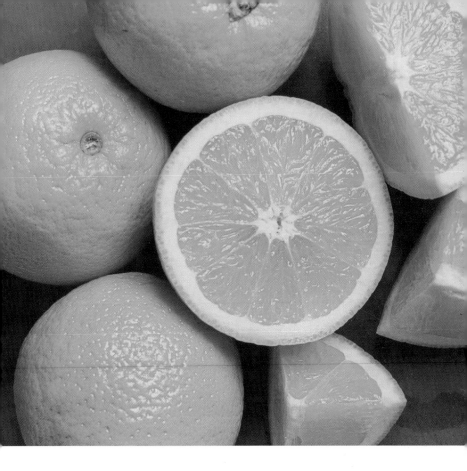

I like oranges.

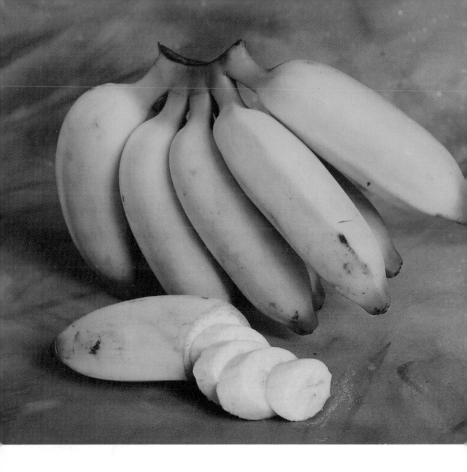

I like bananas.

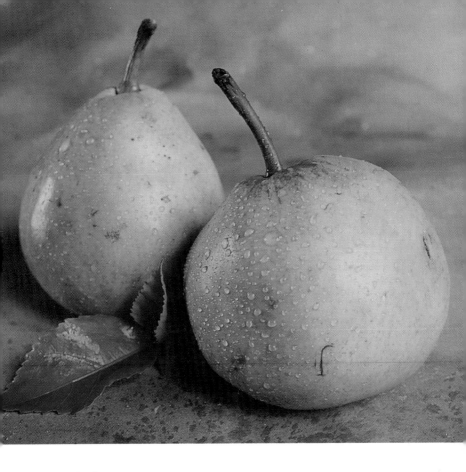

I like pears.

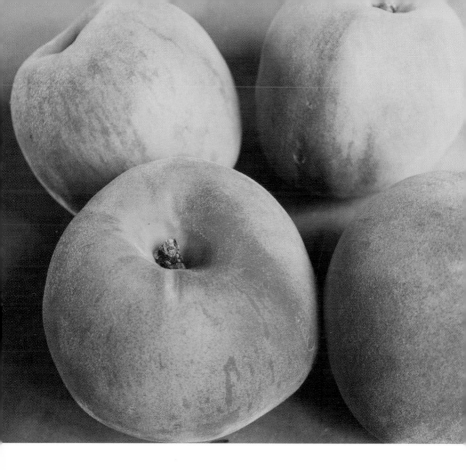

I like peaches.

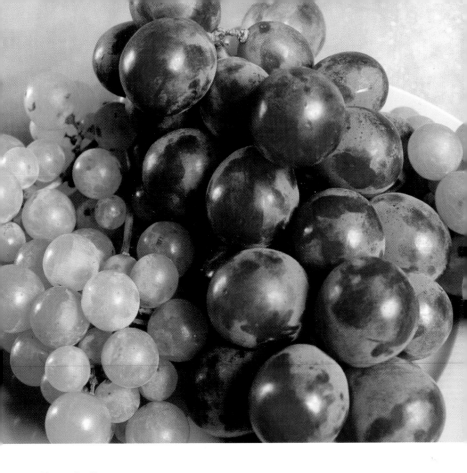

I like grapes.

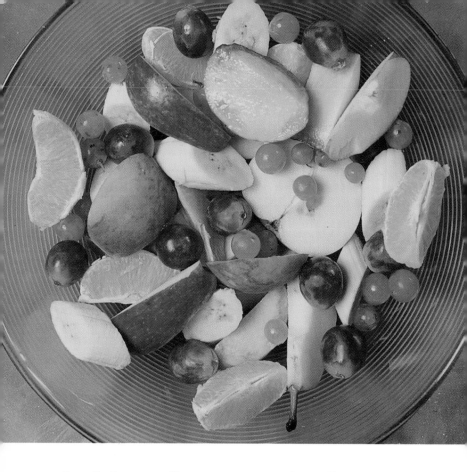

I like fruit salad.